THE
JORDAN RIVER
RULES

THE
JORDAN RIVER
RULES

10 God-Given Strategies
for Moving Forward

Robert J. Morgan

For the Lord your God dried up the water of the Jordan before you until you had crossed over, just as the Lord your God did to the Red Sea.

—JOSHUA 4:23

Cover Design by Brandon Riesgo

Published by Cover to Cover LLC

Hardcover ISBN: 978-0-9884966-4-4

First Edition

Printed in the United States.

To Katrina

Contents

Lord... you hold my future.

—PSALM 16:5

MOVING FORWARD

If the flood gathers, and the Jordan overflows its banks, still the divine watchword, "Forward!" shall speed us on.... God help you to go forward, and unto him be praise for ever and ever. Amen.

—CHARLES HADDON SPURGEON

Years ago, I checked into a hotel and went down the hall to get a soft drink. I fed the vending machine several quarters, but nothing worked, and pounding the machine didn't help. I walked on, looking for another machine, which also took my money. I ventured farther down the hall and found a third machine, but the results were the same, and now I was out of quarters. Suddenly I realized the truth and felt like an idiot. The massive hotel was round, and I'd been walking in circles, putting my coins into the same machine.

It's one thing to do that with loose change; it's another to do it with life.

Millions of people race around, tired, thirsting for significance, collecting some quarters but investing them in things that never satisfy.

Sound like you? Or someone you know?

In the Bible, an entire nation traveled in futile orbits for years—the Children of Israel. If you aren't familiar with the story, here's the short version. According to the book of Exodus, the ancient Israelites were enslaved in Egypt until Moses led them by the power of God through the parted Red Sea. They marched across the desert toward the land God had promised them, pausing at Mount Sinai to receive ten important rules.

The Israelites broke those Ten Commandments before the ink was dry, so to speak. Their grumbling, complaining, moral failure, and unbelief stalled their progress, and God condemned them to forty years of going around in circles.

Four decades passed. Moses, aged and spent, climbed Mount Nebo and died.

Moses' aide, Joshua, took over. He was God's appointed leader to conduct the Israelites out of the wilderness and into their promised homeland. It was a thrilling operation. But first, they had to cross the Jordan River, which was at flood stage; and for that, God duplicated a matchless miracle. He again parted the waters, just as He had split the Red Sea a generation earlier.

Think of it! The travels of the Israelites were bookended by parted waters. At the Red Sea, the same God who led them in, led them out. Forty years later at the Jordan River, the same God who led them out, led them on. He guided them to the next stage of their national life—the Promised Land.

In the 1990s, I was traveling from Athens to America under a cloud of personal difficulty. I had a window seat, and my devotions that day were in Exodus 14. No one sat beside me. I opened my Bible, pulled out a yellow pad, and began taking notes. As I read about the Lord's parting of the Red Sea, the lessons spilled onto my notepad faster than I could record. It's as though the Holy Spirit occupied the empty seat beside me, saying, "Now, here's what you need to know about handling your trouble."

The principles I discovered helped me enormously, and I later hammered them into the little book *The Red Sea Rules*, which has sold more than a half-million copies. That was two decades ago; and in the intervening years, I've continued to study the journeys of the Israelites. The first books of the Bible—Genesis, Exodus, Leviticus, Numbers, and Deuteronomy—tell their story, and much of it occurred under the leadership of Moses. But the next book in the Bible bears the name *Joshua*, and it tells how the Israelites finally claimed their land of promise.

Perhaps you've survived your own Red Sea experiences, when the enemy was strong, the danger great, and the fear deep. God helped you through that, didn't He? He made a way for you when there seemed no way.

Now it's time to move forward toward all the promises He has given you—the Promised Land of a rewarding future. The psalmist said, "LORD, you are my portion and my cup of blessing; you hold my future" (Psalm 16:5).

The same Lord who holds your future also holds you. Don't be hostage to the past. Never get stuck in the desert. Yes, there's value in every past experience, good and bad. You can glean a lot of lessons in the desert, discover a lot of grace, and develop a lot of maturity, but it all equips you for something more.

Everything so far in your life—including your Red Sea moments of crisis—is simply His preparation for stronger days ahead.

That's the lesson of this simple study, which covers the first six chapters of the book of Joshua. I'll not pause at every paragraph in those chapters, but I want to pass on to you some of the rules I've learned when facing the changing events of life—the Jordan River Rules.

This story brims with spiritual significance. Moses, representing the Law, is dead; but Joshua, whose name from Hebrew to English is *Jesus*, is ready to do what Moses could not—lead God's people into the Promised Land. That's to say—Jesus Himself is ready to lead you to a rewarding future, whatever your age, whatever your past, whatever your scars.

Joshua 6:7 says, "Move forward."

It's time to get on with the *rest* of your life and with the *best* of your life. Break out of the wilderness circuit and cross the swollen Jordan to your promised future.

You've got an adventure ahead of you!

The same God who led you in and led you out—He will lead you on.

JORDAN RIVER RULE #1

REALIZE GOD MEANS FOR YOU TO MOVE FORWARD

JOSHUA 1

After the death of Moses the LORD's servant, the LORD spoke to Joshua son of Nun, Moses's assistant: "Moses my servant is dead. Now you and all the people prepare to cross over the Jordan to the land I am giving the Israelites."

—JOSHUA 1:1-2

God Leads
Us In Stages

The book of Joshua is about the victory of faith and the glory that comes to God when His people trust and obey.

—Warren W. Wiersbe

As I began this book, my wife of forty-three years, Katrina, passed away after a long battle with multiple sclerosis. It was Veteran's Day, 2019, and all of us were around her bed. The nurse announced, "The time of death is 11:11 a.m."

Someone said, "She went to heaven at 11:11 on 11/11."

Then my son-in-law pulled out his Bible and said, "Listen to this! In John 11:11, Jesus said, 'Our friend Lazarus has fallen asleep, but I'm on my way to wake him up.'"

I can't describe the comfort I felt—John 11:11 at 11:11 on 11/11!

God has many ways of comforting us, yet new chapters are difficult. I'm aware my life is entering a new phase, and I'm reminded life unfolds in stages. The stages may be bittersweet; but, as Katrina would have reminded me, it's important to keep a positive biblical attitude. The day after she went to heaven, my daily Bible reading took me to the first chapter of Joshua, where I read:

> After the death of Moses the Lord's servant, the Lord spoke to Joshua son of Nun, Moses's assistant: "Moses my servant is dead. Now you and all the people prepare to cross over the Jordan to the land I am giving the Israelites. I have given you every place where the sole of your foot treads, just as I promised Moses. Your territory will be from the wilderness and Lebanon to the great river, the Euphrates River—all the land of the Hittites—and west to the Mediterranean Sea. No one will be able to stand against you as long as you live. I will be with you, just as I was with Moses. I will not leave you or abandon you." (Joshua 1:1-5)

This passage provides three truths about God's guidance: He leads us in stages; He leads us in steps; and He leads us in Person. The idea of stages is introduced earlier, in the book of Numbers, which Moses wrote near the end of the Israelites' years of wandering.

Numbers 33:1-2 says: "These were the **stages** of the Israelites' journey when they went out of the land of Egypt…. At the LORD's command, Moses wrote down the starting points for the **stages** of their journey; these are the **stages** listed by their starting points."[1]

Three times we're told God led the Israelites in stages; and when we turn the page to Joshua 1:1, they're entering another—one that brought both mourning and momentum. The Lord told the Israelites of the death of Moses, the only leader they'd ever known. New stages in life often involve mourning. But they also involve morning. They represent new days in our lives. Psalm 84:5-7 says: "Happy are the people whose strength is in you, whose hearts are set on pilgrimage.... They go from strength to strength."

My life has passed through a series of stages—from a youngster in a happy home, to a college student away from home, to a young single, to a husband, a father, a grandfather. From the pastor of a smaller church to the pastor of a larger church. From a pastor to a writer and speaker. And now to a widower. Each stage has bewildered me at first. But the Lord has given me strength for every stage. Everything is under His control and orchestrated in His timing.

Are you on the border of a new stage in life?

Maybe a graduation, a wedding, a divorce, a birth, a death, a new job, an illness, a recovery, a new home, a move, a breakup, a new relationship, a new church, a change of some sort? Many transitions are stressful and bring mixed emotions. It's all right to feel sadness, regret, grief, confusion, or relief. But turn yourself around and head in a positive direction. Don't get stuck in negative moods or hopeless inertia.

Actress Lauren Bacall once said, "I am not a has-been. I am a will-be."[2]

The apostle Paul put it better: "But one thing I do: Forgetting what is behind and reaching forward to what is ahead, I pursue as my goal the prize promised by God's heavenly call in Christ Jesus. Therefore, let all of us who are mature think this way" (Philippians 3:13-15).

Mature people think that way! I miss Katrina constantly, and I'll catch up to her one day soon. But I'm determined to go forward.

Prepare for what God is preparing for you. Your next stage in life is God-planned. The One who knows the way through the wilderness also knows the way into the Promised Land.

God Leads
Us In Steps

I have given you every place where the sole of your foot treads, just as I promised Moses.

—Joshua 1:3

Life unfolds in stages, but we take it in steps.

As a follower of Jesus Christ, I'm convinced God has an agenda for my life with every detail prearranged from eternity past. That knowledge changes the way I rise each morning and retire each evening. It affects the way I plan my time, establish my priorities, spend my money, and think about my future.

- The psalmist prayed, "All my days were written in your book and planned before a single one of them began" (Psalm 139:16).

- Ephesians 2:10 says, "For we are his workmanship, created in Christ Jesus for good works, which God prepared ahead of time for us to do."

I recently talked with a friend back from military service in a dangerous area. His mission reminded me of a commando show I'm watching on television. Coming home, he said, is a huge adjustment. Gone is the danger, the adrenaline, the sense of purpose, the intensity. Now he's back to raking leaves and running errands. The change is dramatic, but I've sought to remind him God plans our days. Some days I'm preaching to five thousand people and other days I'm cleaning the sink and doing the laundry. The important thing is fulfilling what God has called me to do that day.

When Moses led the Israelites out of bondage and Joshua assumed control on the banks of the Jordan River, the Lord said to them, "I have given you every place where the sole of your foot treads, just as I promised" (Joshua 1:3).

The only way of moving forward is putting your foot down—and making sure it lands on a promise. You can never claim Joshua 1:3 by standing still. You have to go forward, along the pathway of God's promises.

Not too long ago, I spoke at Beulah Heights University. In studying the history of the school, I learned of two of its alumni, Nolan and Dorothy Lee, who attended in the 1940s. It was a new stage for them and they lived on leftovers from the school dining hall. Nolan milked cows and Dorothy cleaned restrooms to earn money. One day, when there was nothing to eat, she put her Bible on the floor and carefully stepped on it. She said, "Lord, I am standing on Your Word and Your promises to provide for us." Finishing her prayer, she heard a rustle at the door and found two grocery bags of food.[3]

Somewhere I read of a mother who wrote Bible promises on slips of paper, folded them, and put them in her children's shoes. In this way she taught them to "walk by faith."

I've never stood on the Bible or put verses in my shoes, but I do believe Psalm 119:105: "Your word is a lamp for my feet and a light on my path."

As I'm facing a new stage in my life, here's what it means for me. Every morning, I take time to read my Bible and pray. I ask the Lord to show me what He wants me to do that day, and I walk by faith, step by step, into the Promised Land of His good will for my life.

You can do the same.

So put your foot down, make sure to plant it on a promise, and take the next step!

GOD LEADS US IN PERSON

I will be with you, just as I was with Moses. I will not leave you or abandon you.

—JOSHUA 1:5

About a month before Katrina passed away, I lifted her into bed and we prayed together. Then I went outside and sat on the patio, tired and troubled. Out of nowhere, an old song came to mind. Pulling out my phone, I looked it up and listened to it. I hadn't heard it for years, but it captured my heart. The next day, I had to rush Katrina to the emergency room, and that was the beginning of the final phase of her disease. Throughout the entire month, this song was a soundtrack in my mind.

> I trust in God wherever I may be,
> Upon the land or on the rolling sea;
> For come what may, from day to day,
> My heavenly Father watches over me.[4]

Whenever you enter a new phase, your Heavenly Father watches over you. He shows up in Person to lead you. For me, it means I'll never come home to an empty house or enter a vacant room. The God of heaven is near. I most intimately sense the Lord's presence when I'm alone with Him in Bible study and prayer. Jesus told us to shut the door and spend time with our Father in secret (Matthew 6:6). But when we exit the room and plunge into the day, we don't leave the Father behind. Dr. Gregory Boyd wrote, "I've become absolutely convinced that remaining aware of God's presence is the single most important task in the life of every follower of Jesus."[5]

Recently I spoke to Christian workers in Asia, and after the talk, a young man came up and hugged me as if I were his father. I asked where he was from, and he named a dangerous and unstable country. I asked what he did.

"I evangelize terrorists," he said. "I live in [redacted]. But the people there have souls, and they also have families and children. I'm seeking to bring the message of Christ to them."

"Isn't it dangerous?" I asked.

"Yes."

"Are you afraid?"

"No," he said, looking surprised I would ask. "I have the Holy Spirit with me!"

If you're walking with God, you have the Holy Spirit with you. That should make a big difference, shouldn't it?

God's promise that He will never leave us or forsake us is very special. This remarkable combination of verbs, *I will never leave you or abandon you,* occurs several times in Scripture.

You'll find this phrase in Deuteronomy 31 in verses 6 and 8. Here it is again in Joshua 1:5. David quotes it in 1 Chronicles 28:20, and he turns it into a prayer in Psalm 27:9.

Then the writer of Hebrews snatches it from the pages of the Old Testament and presents it this way: "Be satisfied with what you have, for he himself has said, I will never leave you or abandon you" (Hebrews 13:5).

In the Greek text of Hebrews, the word "leave" is preceded by a double negative: "Never, never will I leave you." The word "abandon" is preceded by three negatives: "Never, never, never will I abandon you." This Greek construction of Hebrews 13:5 is reflected in the final stanza of one of my favorite hymns, "How Firm a Foundation," which says:

> The soul that on Jesus has leaned for repose,
> I will not, I will not desert to its foes;
> That soul, though all hell should endeavor
> to shake,
> I'll never, no never, no never forsake.

Why on Earth, then, are you and I ever insecure about anything in our lives? We have rivers to cross, challenges to face, problems to confront, giants to fight, and promises to claim. But why should we be insecure, afraid, or discouraged? We have a repeated promise from God, and the final repetition of it is underlined by doubles and triples of grace.

God leads us in stages, in steps, and in Person, and He will never leave us or forsake us. Remind yourself of these truths from Joshua 1:1-5, and don't be afraid of the next stage or step. Whatever comes or wherever you may be, your Heavenly Father watches over you.

For individual and group study materials, including videos and study guides, and for discounts on bulk purchases, visit jordanriverrules.com

JORDAN RIVER RULE #2

SAY NO TO DISCOURAGEMENT, YES TO STRENGTH

JOSHUA 1:6-9

Haven't I commanded you: be strong and courageous? Do not be afraid or discouraged, for the Lord your God is with you wherever you go.

—JOSHUA 1:9

BE STRONG

Strong faith glorifies God because it treats Him as God.

—CHARLES H. SPURGEON

The opening verses of the book of Joshua are some of the most bracing words in the Bible. They've energized God's people for the last three millennia, and they've been cherished verses of mine for the last fifty years, recently more than ever. Joshua 1:6 begins with the command, "Be strong."

During my wife's final days, I needed to be strong for her and my family. Near the end, I wanted to whisper in her ear that I loved her, and we'd meet in the morning and stroll alongside the Crystal River. I was making a date with her. For a moment, the words wouldn't come; my emotions overwhelmed me. But I glanced up at the iron bed frame, focused on the black metal, forced my thoughts into line, and found strength from God.

After returning from her graveside, I studied the command to "be strong" in Scripture and found it occurred exactly thirty times—one for just about every day of the month.

Be strong and courageous; don't be terrified or afraid of them. For the Lord…will go with you.
—Deuteronomy 31:6

Be strong and courageous. —Deuteronomy 31:7

The LORD commissioned Joshua son of Nun, "Be strong and courageous." —Deuteronomy 31:23

Be strong and courageous. —Joshua 1:6

*Above all, **be strong** and very courageous to observe carefully the whole instruction my servant Moses commanded you.* —Joshua 1:7

*Haven't I commanded you: **be strong** and courageous?* —Joshua 1:9

*Above all, **be strong** and courageous!* —Joshua 1:18

*Do not be afraid or discouraged. **Be strong** and courageous, for the Lord will do this.* —Joshua 10:25

Be strong! Let's prove ourselves strong for our people and for the cities of our God. May the Lord's will be done. —2 Samuel 10:12

Be strong and valiant!—2 Samuel 13:28

Be strong and be a man. —1 Kings 2:2

Be strong *and courageous. Don't be afraid or discouraged.* —1 Chronicles 22:13

The Lord has chosen you to build a house for the sanctuary. ***Be strong****, and do it.* —1 Chronicles 28:10

Be strong *and courageous, and do the work. Don't be afraid or discouraged, for the Lord God...is with you. He won't leave you or abandon you until all the work for the service of the Lord's house is finished.* —1 Chronicles 28:20

But as for you, ***be strong****; don't give up, for your work has a reward.* —2 Chronicles 15:7

Be strong*; may the Lord be with those who do what is good.* —2 Chronicles 19:11

Be strong *for battle!* —2 Chronicles 25:8

Be strong *and courageous! Don't be afraid or discouraged before the king of Assyria or before the large army that is with him, for there are more with us than with him.* —2 Chronicles 32:7

Be strong *and take action!* —Ezra 10:4

Wait for the Lord; ***be strong****, and let your heart be courageous.* —Psalm 27:14

***Be strong**, and let your heart be courageous, all you who put your hope in the Lord.* —Psalm 31:24

*Say to the cowardly: "**Be strong**; do not fear! Here is your God."* —Isaiah 35:4

*The people who know their God will **be strong** and take action.* —Daniel 11:32

*Even so, **be strong**, Zerubbabel.* —Haggai 2:4

***Be strong**, Joshua son of Jehozadak, high priest.* —Haggai 2:4

***Be strong**, all you people of the land…. Work! For I am with you.* —Haggai 2:4

*Let your hands **be strong**.* —Zechariah 8:9

*You will be a blessing. Don't be afraid; let your hands **be strong**.* —Zechariah 8:13

*Be alert, stand firm in the faith, be courageous, **be strong**.* —1 Corinthians 16:13

*You, therefore, my son, **be strong** in the grace that is in Christ Jesus.* —2 Timothy 2:1

You can't conjure up strength like a wizard summoning a genie. It comes from meditating on words like these. Joshua 1:8 tells us to meditate on Scripture day and night. As you do so, you'll learn our Lord is all powerful. There's no exhausting of His might, no diminishing of His power, no ebbing of His fortitude.

Choose, through grace, to be enthusiastic. Take the thirty "be strong" verses as your personal slogans of strength. Write a different one atop every page of the calendar. Learn some of them by heart. Meditate on them. Weave them into your thoughts until they animate your personality. One of the secrets of amassing strength is reminding yourself God requires it—and He who requires it, provides it.

Do Not Be Afraid

---

*Be strong and courageous…. be strong and very courageous….
Do not be afraid.*

—Joshua 1:6-9

George Washington's mother, Mary, was a pillar of strength despite loss and sorrow. She was orphaned as a child, later widowed, and she raised five children alone. Mary placed her faith in Christ and was buoyed by reading the Bible and her cherished collection of devotional books.

Nonetheless, Mary was given to anxiety. She worried about George in combat. She fretted about finances. And from childhood, Mary was terrified of storms. Once in her old age, a thunderstorm blew in while Mary was staying with her daughter. Betty found her mother upstairs kneeling in prayer. Mary confessed she had been "striving for years against this weakness, for you know, Betty, my trust is in God; but sometimes my fears are stronger than my faith."[6]

How we know it! Nothing is more agonizing than anxiety. It's what kept the Israelites in the wilderness forty

19

years. In Numbers 13, Moses sent twelve scouts to spy the land for the invasion of Canaan. That's when everything went wrong. "We went into the land where you sent us," they reported. "Indeed it is flowing with milk and honey…. However, the people living in the land are strong, and the cities are large and fortified…. We can't attack the people because they are stronger than we are!" (Numbers 13:27-31).

Their fears were stronger than their faith, and that marred their future. Now forty years later, the Israelites were back in the same place under a new leader, and the Lord warned them seven times against the same mistake, telling them, "Do not be afraid."

> *Be strong and courageous;* **don't be terrified or afraid**. —Deuteronomy 31:6

> **Do not be afraid.** —Deuteronomy 31:8

> **Do not be afraid.** —Joshua 1:9

> *The Lord said to Joshua,* **"Do not be afraid."** —Joshua 8:1

> *The Lord said to Joshua,* **"Do not be afraid** *of them."* —Joshua 10:8

*Joshua said to them, **"Do not be afraid."***
—Joshua 10:25

*The LORD said to Joshua, **"Do not be afraid."***
—Joshua 11:6[7]

Those words are for you as much as for Joshua. Woven into them is a Scriptural formula—fear is overestimating your problems and underestimating your God. How often we minimize our Savior and maximize our storms!

This is no little matter. The future isn't easy. Jesus said, "Each day has enough trouble of its own" (Matthew 6:34), and He told us, "You will have suffering in this world" (John 16:33). If we focus on the stresses, we'll be distressed. If we focus on Christ, we'll be confident. It's a matter of gripping His promises instead of griping about our problems.

In essence, fear is the sin of forgetfulness—forgetting the fathomless omnipotence of the Lord Christ and His truth. When that happens, our anxieties become a cycle of inefficient thoughts spinning through our heads like a whirlwind. Accept challenges as they come, but don't magnify them. Magnify *Him*, and He will give you the land.

Do Not Be Discouraged

Haven't I commanded you: be strong and courageous? Do not be afraid or discouraged.

—Joshua 1:9

The Bible has nothing good to say about discouragement. Not one word. Not a single verse commending discouragement, touting its virtue, or advocating its adoption. Like dishonesty or immorality, discouragement is a wrong choice. It's a sin.

The ten spies were condemned for "discouraging the Israelites from crossing into the land the LORD has given them" (Numbers 32:7).

In the book of Joshua, you'll find three commands against discouragement (Joshua 1:9; 8:1; and 10:25). In 1 Samuel 17:32, David saw how demoralized the Israelites were because of Goliath, and he told King Saul, "Don't let anyone be discouraged by him; your servant will go and fight this Philistine!"

David later told his son Solomon, "Don't be afraid or discouraged" (1 Chronicles 22:13 and 28:20).

When King Jehoshaphat was in danger, the voice of the prophet rang out: "Do not be afraid or discouraged because of this vast number, for the battle is not yours, but God's…. Do not be afraid or discouraged" (2 Chronicles 20:15-17).

King Hezekiah told Israel during another national crisis, "Be strong and courageous! Don't be…discouraged" (2 Chronicles 32:7).

Isaiah said the Messiah "will not grow weak or be discouraged until he has established justice on earth" (Isaiah 42:4).

The Lord told the prophet Ezekiel regarding the wicked, "Don't be…discouraged by the look on their faces" (Ezekiel 2:6).

In the Gospels, the two disciples of Emmaus were downcast and "looked discouraged" (Luke 24:17). They soon learned their discouragement was a waste of energy, for they were walking alongside the risen Savior.

Ephesians 3:13 says, "I ask you not to be discouraged."

We're told to "comfort the discouraged" in 1 Thessalonians 5:14.

Discouragement comes when Satan siphons away your stamina. It's the germ of gloom that sends the plague of pessimism through your bloodstream, and it's highly contagious. When I succumb to discouragement, it pulls down those around me.

When I'm discouraged, it's because I'm looking at myself, my own goals, my hopes and aspirations, my dreams and drives. Whenever I'm encouraged, it's because I'm looking at the Lord and His plans and purposes.

Here are three suggestions for overcoming discouragement.

First, **resignation**. Give God the aspirations you're clinging to; He can do more with them than you can. Let's surrender our dreams and desires to God and say with Jacob, "If I am bereaved, I am bereaved" (Genesis 43:14, NIV). Or with Esther, "If I perish, I perish" (Esther 4:16). Or with Job, "Even if he kills me, I will hope in him" (Job 13:15). Or with Jesus, "Yet not as I will, but as you will" (Matthew 26:39).

Second, **recalibration**. Expect God to turn blows into blessings and setbacks into comebacks. He produces glory for Himself through life's misfortunes. Early in ministry, I became discouraged because the church down the street had more than two thousand people each Sunday, while I had less than two hundred. I slowly realized my success had nothing to do with the size of my ministry and everything to do with working joyfully each day as God directed.

Third, **recalculation**. We have to count our blessings and add up our gains. In any situation, we can find things for which to be thankful. Try this experiment. Tonight when you go to bed, make a short list of all the problems, failures, and upsets you faced during the day and think about them as you go to sleep. Tomorrow night, make a short list of all the blessings and benefits you experienced during the day, and go to bed thanking God for those.

Which left you in better shape?

Press ahead into whatever God has for you and take these words to heart: *Be strong and courageous! Do not be afraid! Do not be discouraged!* Galvanize yourself against gloom by the inoculation of God's grace. That's the only safe passage forward.

For individual and group study materials, including videos and study guides, and for discounts on bulk purchases, visit jordanriverrules.com

Jordan River Rule #3

Step Up to
the Moment

Joshua 1:10-18

Get provisions ready for yourselves, for within three days you will be crossing the Jordan to go in and take possession of the land the Lord your God is giving you to inherit.

—Joshua 1:11

DON'T MESS UP NOW

Earth's saddest day and gladdest day were just three days apart!

—SUSAN COOLIDGE

Many years ago, Katrina and I ministered in Japan, and we purchased a set of Asian tea cups for our daughter, Victoria. They were fragile, and I went to a lot of trouble to hand-carry them home, tucking them carefully into the overhead bins or under the seat on the plane and making sure I didn't drop them in the airports. When we arrived home, Victoria came over to see us. I pulled out her china and started to hand a teacup to her. It slipped from my fingers and broke to pieces on the dining room table. I had carried that cup 6,638 miles but dropped it the last twelve inches of the way.

The Children of Israel had traveled forty years from Egypt and through the wilderness, and Joshua didn't want them messing up so close to the completion of their journey. He told them, "Get provisions ready for yourselves, for within three days you will be crossing the Jordan to go in and take possession of the land the Lord your God is giving you to inherit" (Joshua 1:11).

It's easy to mess up between stages of life. I know a lot of people who lift their foot from the gas, take a needless detour, or take their eyes off the road—and they don't make it safely home. I'm not talking about driving but about the journey of life.

Along these lines, I've noticed something in the Bible. The people of God often took three days to rest and prepare for the next stage. Three literal days.

In Genesis 42, Joseph's brothers came to Egypt seeking grain. Joseph recognized them and knew God was going to do something to restore his family; but Joseph wanted time for his brothers to examine their hearts, so he put them into jail for three days (Genesis 42:17).

In 1 Chronicles 12:39, David's men ate and drank and celebrated three days when proclaiming him king of Israel.

When Ezra gathered the exiles at the Ahava River to travel to Jerusalem, they spent three days preparing and praying and fasting (Ezra 8:15). Upon arriving in Jerusalem, they spent three days resting and preparing for their next steps (Ezra 8:32).

When Nehemiah made a similar trek from Persia to Jerusalem, he too rested for three days, preparing for his task of rebuilding the walls of Jerusalem (Nehemiah 2:11).

When Queen Esther realized she had to champion the cause of her endangered Jewish race before King Ahasuerus, she and Mordecai fasted and prepared for three days before implementing their plan (Esther 4:16).

When God wanted to change Jonah's heart, He detained him three days in the stomach of a great fish (Jonah 1:17).

When the Lord Jesus wanted to find His Father's will for His life as a twelve-year-old, He stayed behind in Jerusalem for three days—to the distress of His parents (Luke 2:46).

When God wanted to bring about a remarkable change in the heart of Saul of Tarsus, He left him blind three days (Acts 9:9). Later, after Saul of Tarsus had become the apostle Paul, he finally made it to his ultimate destination of Rome. But before engaging in ministry, he took three days for rest and prayer (Acts 28:17).

Before Cornelius and his household came to Christ, which extended the Gospel to the Gentiles and created the global Church, the Lord kept him waiting and praying three days for Peter's arrival (Acts 10:30, NIV).

And of course, the Lord Jesus spent three days in the tomb—and His disciples spent three days in sober reflection before the dawning of the greatest day that ever was—Easter Sunday!

I'm not saying there is a kind of spiritual magic about three days. But before we enter any new endeavor, we want to prepare ourselves spiritually. We need some time in prayer, in thinking, perhaps in fasting, perhaps in resting. We need some time to linger in God's presence and to get ready for what He has for us. We've come too far to mess up now.

If you're able to do so, before making a major decision or undertaking a significant task, take "three days" and spend some time praying, pondering, worshiping, and resting. Resting can lead to poise and purpose. Rushing can lead to rash decisions and impulsive actions.

Take a deep breath, be still, remember He is God, seek first His Kingdom, and get ready to step up to the moment.

EVERYTHING... EVERYWHERE

Anywhere, provided it be forward!

—MARY SLESSOR, PIONEER MISSIONARY TO NIGERIA

The future nation of Israel was a confederation of twelve tribes that had descended from the twelve sons of Jacob. As the people massed on the plains of Moab preparing to ford the Jordan River and possess their Promised Land, Joshua visited three of the tribes—Reuben, Gad, and Manasseh. Moses had told these tribes they could possess lands on the eastern side of the Jordan River in the area now known as the nations of Jordan and Syria. After all, the boundary of Israel was ideally to extend from the Euphrates River to the Mediterranean Sea (Exodus 23:31).

The other nine tribes would have to fight for their land on the west bank of the river—the territory now known as the West Bank and the nation of Israel. But there was a stipulation to the agreement. The armies of Reuben, Gad, and Manasseh had to fully deploy with the others in crossing the Jordan, defeating Jericho, and subduing the Promised Land.

General Joshua wanted to avoid any problems with this agreement. As the nine tribes prepared for the conquest, he gathered the leaders of Reuben, Gad, and Manasseh and told them, "Your wives, dependents, and livestock may remain in the land Moses gave you on this side of the Jordan. But your best soldiers must cross over in battle formation ahead of your brothers and help them" (Joshua 1:14).

They answered Joshua, "Everything you have commanded us we will do, and everywhere you send us we will go" (Joshua 1:16).

Whenever I read this, I remember that the name *Joshua* is, in the original Hebrew text, *Yeshua*. In the Greek, it is *Iesous*, which, in English, is *Jesus*.

In preparing for the next stages of life, it's vital to say to Jesus, "Everything You have commanded me I will do, and everywhere You send me I will go."

My college years were spent at Columbia International University, which celebrated the Victorious Christian Life. The school's president at the time, Dr. Robertson McQuilkin, told us:

> What glorious good news! No matter what may or may not have occurred in the past and no matter how inadequate my understanding, if my relationship to God is one of unconditional surrender and confident expec-

tation that He will keep His word, I can experience a life of consistent victory over temptation and growth toward His own likeness, I can see His purpose for my ministry supernaturally fulfilled, and above all, I can daily experience loving companionship with my Savior.[8]

That says it all!

Our future isn't a matter of our own autonomous ambition. It's a matter of submission to the perfect will of God. There's no point going forward if it's down the wrong path. We aren't on earth long, and all is wasted by a self-focused life. We must deny ourselves, take up our cross, follow Him, and say, "Lord, not my will but Yours be done—whatever You tell me, wherever You send me."

Missionary Hudson Taylor said, "Let us give up our work, our thoughts, our plans, ourselves, our lives, our loved ones, our influence, our all, right into His hand, and then, when we have given all over to Him, there will be nothing left for us to be troubled about, or to make trouble about."[9]

That's the only way of stepping up to the moment and seizing the future.

Earlier this year, I studied Psalm 37:4: "Take delight in the Lord, and he will give you your heart's desires." I had always interpreted that to mean if we delight ourselves in the Lord, He will fulfill our desires. But there's a better interpretation. If we make the Lord our heart's delight, He will place within us the desires we most need in our hearts and which will bring us greatest joy.

Everything changes when God has all there is of us to have. As one of my professors put it, "All there is of God is available to the person who is available to all there is of God."[10]

For individual and group study materials, including videos and study guides, and for discounts on bulk purchases, visit jordanriverrules.com

JORDAN RIVER
RULE #4

FIND SOMEONE TO
HELP ALONG THE WAY

JOSHUA 2

We will show kindness and faithfulness to you when the Lord gives us the land.

—JOSHUA 2:14

The Spies and the Prostitute

*The gift of kindness may start as a small ripple that over time
can turn into a tidal wave affecting the lives of many.*

—Kevin Heath

Two young men crept out of the camp as stealthily as leopards. They were Israeli spies, lean and fit and smart. Fording the Jordan, they saw before them the towering walls of Jericho. The gates were open and streams of people, donkeys, camels, children, and wagons were coming and going like a never-ending parade. The spies missed nothing—the guards, the fortifications, the reinforcements. They joined the crowds, entered the city, and looked for a place where visiting men wouldn't be out of place—a brothel.

Prostitution in Jericho was probably considered an honorable enterprise. According to Genesis 15:16, the Lord waited four hundred years for the sins of the Canaanites to reach full measure. Every generation sunk a little lower than the preceding one. The entire city was now beyond redemption, except a harlot's family.

Guided by Providence, it was Rahab's house the spies entered. She'd heard rumors about the Israelites, and she knew the stories of the parting of the Red Sea. Perhaps from her window she could see their massed encampment beyond the Jordan, and she yearned to know their God.

Officers traced the route of the spies and began pounding on the door. Rahab led the two men up narrow steps to the roof where bundles of flax were spread as thick as a mown harvest. "Hide here," she said, and she literally buried the men beneath piles of crops.

As night fell, Rahab tiptoed back to the roof, pulled the men from the flax, and whispered: "I know that the Lord has given you this land…. for the Lord your God is God in heaven above and on earth below. Now please swear to me by the Lord that you will also show kindness to my father's family, because I showed kindness to you. Give me a sure sign that you will spare the lives of my father, mother, brothers, sisters, and all who belong to them, and save us from death" (Joshua 2:9-13).

The two young men saw a crimson rope coiled in the corner and told her to tie it to the window, marking her house for deliverance when the day of conquest arrived. That's exactly what happened. When the city of Jericho was destroyed a few days later, Rahab and her family were saved.

There is a lesson here. As they went about their dangerous mission, the two young men managed to find someone who helped them and whom they could help along the way.

As we move into the upcoming stages in our lives, we need to receive and give help, and that's part of our mission. God, in His providence, puts souls in our pathways, and we'll find even a small act of kindness creates a ripple that, as time goes by, affects many and takes on a life of its own.

Who would have imagined that a profligate prostitute and two hardened Israeli spies would, during a dangerous military mission, exchange acts of kindness that would change history? Rahab later married an Israeli man named Salmon (was he one of the spies?), and they had a son named Boaz, who later married Ruth. Their son was Obed, who had a son named Jesse, whose youngest boy, David, became the king of Israel and the forefather of Jesus Christ.

That's why you find Rahab's name in the fifth verse of the New Testament—Matthew 1:5—in the genealogy of Christ. Rahab is also mentioned two other times in the New Testament. Hebrews 11:31 says, "By faith Rahab the prostitute welcomed the spies in peace and didn't perish with those who disobeyed." And James 2:25 says, "In the same way, wasn't Rahab the prostitute also justified by works in receiving the messengers and sending them out by a different route?"

You never know when the smallest acts of kindness will yield some of the biggest surprises in history. So find someone to help along the way!

THE CATHEDRAL WINDOW

Every scrap of kindness is more than it seams.

—AN UNKNOWN QUILTER

My mother, Edith Morgan, was a schoolteacher, home-maker, and quilter. I have one of her handsewn quilts—a "cathedral window"—at the foot of my bed. Though her handiwork was painstaking and priceless, I never knew her to sell one of her quilts. They went to friends and family, and a few were stored in the closet for generations unborn.

When she passed away in 2000, Mom left behind a chest full of remnants, all cut and colorful, squared and ready to go. She didn't expect to die yet, and she was planning her next project. Quilting kept the winter blues at bay. But with her passing, those final remnants stayed in the darkness of the old chest in the attic, seeing a flash of light only when a curious grandchild opened the lid for a moment.

Two decades passed and then came the coronavirus pandemic.

Mom's granddaughter, Sara, a nurse, treated COVID patients in a hospital that ran out of facemasks. Sara called her mother requesting help, and my sister Ann drove to our homeplace, opened the chest, and piled the remnants into a basket. Returning home, she took her needle and thread and began making miniature quilts of her own—face masks.

It was a legacy of leftovers. My mother could never have imagined how her assortment of carefully cut squares would be used. I'm reminded of Aesop's words: "No act of kindness, no matter how small, is ever wasted."

We can all become masked strangers committing indiscriminate acts of kindness as we help someone along the way. A smile. A "God bless you." An encouraging note or phone call. An extra gift to the charity we support. A salute to a police officer. A wave to an emergency responder. A prayer for our neighbor. A plate of cookies to a grief-stricken friend. An apology. A tap on the brake to let a car merge in front of us.

Let's blanket our world with patience, kindness, and self-sacrifice. No scrap of sympathy is ever wasted, for God knows all the odds and ends of our decency. Our lives are not simply a mishmash of loose threads; they are preplanned and precious. Our deeds echo into the future, even beyond our own span of days. Almighty God knows how to stitch the remnants of our experiences into cathedral windows. The kind things we do take on a life of their own—and only eternity will tell the full story.

As my mom well knew, a life hemmed in kindness will never unravel.

THE CRIMSON CORD

This crimson cord of salvation, saving both the spies and Rahab's family, represented, in this strangely typical history, the saving blood of our Lord Jesus.

—HOWARD CROSBY

On that dangerous evening in ancient Jericho, a prostitute and two spies exchanged acts of kindness. At the risk of her life, Rahab hid them. And at the risk of their lives, they promised to come back and rescue her and her family. But there was one condition—the crimson rope. In the fog and fury of the impending war, finding and rescuing one family from the melee would be difficult. So the spies gave specific instructions: "When we enter the land, you tie this scarlet cord to the window through which you let us down. Bring your father, mother, brothers, and all your father's family into your house" (Joshua 2:18).

Rahab lowered them down the wall by a rope—maybe the same crimson cord. It saved the spies; and within a few days, it saved her family too.

The crimson cord was to Rahab what the blood of the Passover lamb was to the Israelites forty years earlier as they painted the crimson color onto their doorposts. And who can ponder this scene without thinking of the crimson blood of our Passover Lamb, who is our scarlet rope of deliverance?

The Bible is the story of this trail of blood, from the blood of the slain Abel, to the sacrificial lambs of the temple, to the redemptive wounds of Christ on the cross. We are "justified by his blood" (Romans 5:9), we have "redemption through his blood" (Ephesians 1:7), and His blood cleanses "our consciences from dead works so that we can serve the living God" (Hebrews 9:14). We have boldness to enter God's presence "through the blood of Jesus" (Hebrews 10:19), and the Bible calls it "the precious blood of Christ, like that of an unblemished and spotless lamb" (1 Peter 1:19). When we're cut, our blood *stains* whatever it touches; but the Lord's precious blood *bleaches* whomever it contacts. It is:

- A medicine that cures us from every everlasting ill.

- An acid that burns away our deepest stains.

- An ointment that heals our deepest scars.

- The fuel of our faith.

- The liniment of life.

- An elixir for joy.

- A lotion for peace.

- A vaccine that immunizes us against all the diseases of the devil.

- A fountain filled with blood drawn from Immanuel's veins, where sinners plunged beneath that blood lose all their guilty stains.

The crimson cord that saved Rahab represents the greatest kindness in the universe—God's eternal kindness to us. That's why, in His name and for His glory, our job as we go forward each day is to help someone else along the way in Jesus' name.

For individual and group study materials, including videos and study guides, and for discounts on bulk purchases, visit jordanriverrules.com

Jordan River Rule #5

Expect God to Guide You Where You've Never Been Before

Joshua 3:1-4

When you see the ark of the covenant of the Lord your God carried by the Levitical priests, you are to break camp and follow it.… for you haven't traveled this way before.

—Joshua 3:3-4

THREE-QUARTERS OF A MILE

This must be all their care, to attend the motions of the ark, and follow it with an implicit faith. Thus must we walk after the rule of the word and the direction of the Spirit in every thing.

—MATTHEW HENRY

The Earth weighs approximately 6.6 sextillion tons and is nearly 25,000 miles in circumference at its equator. While the average temperature on Earth is a brisk 59 degrees Fahrenheit, it can range anywhere from 140 degrees in the Libyan Desert to 140 below zero at the South Pole.[11]

Until modern times, much of the Earth's 196,800,000 square miles was uncharted. That changed in the 1800s with the Golden Age of exploration, when a gallery of almost unbelievable men and women raced one another to the ends of the Earth.

In his book *The Explorers,* Martin Dugard suggests we can learn a lot about ourselves by studying these nineteenth-century adventurers, writing, "In our lives, we all move forward into the unknown, making each of us just one of the seven billion explorers on the planet…. There is an explorer within each of us, silently longing to climb our own personal Everest."[12]

That's the theme of *The Jordan River Rules.* We need to move onward into the unexplored future, which can be as daunting as dark continents, blazing deserts, and hostile jungles. But the future is not uncertain to God. He knows tomorrow as well as yesterday, and He delights in leading us where we've never gone before.

Hebrews 11:8 says, "By faith Abraham, when he was called, obeyed and set out for a place that he was going to receive as an inheritance. He went out, even though he did not know where he was going."

Four hundred years later, the descendants of Abraham were doing the same. Joshua 3 begins:

Joshua started early the next morning and left the Acacia Grove with all the Israelites. They went as far as the Jordan and stayed there before crossing. After three days the officers went through the camp and commanded the people, "When you see the ark of the covenant of the Lord your God carried by the Levitical priests, you are to break camp and follow it. But keep a distance of about a thousand yards between yourselves and the ark. Don't go near it, so that you can see the way to go, for you haven't traveled this way before." (Joshua 3:1-4)

The Israelites were no longer wanderers; they were explorers. Their sextant was the ark of the covenant, the mysterious chest that normally resided in the Holy of Holies in the Tabernacle. It represented the earthly footstool of the heavenly throne (1 Chronicles 28:2).

Indeed, it represented the presence of Jesus among them, for the ark was a type of Christ. It was a chest of acacia wood, overlaid with gold both inside and outside (typifying the divinity and humanity of Christ). It was a little longer than a yard, two-and-a-quarter feet wide, and just more than two feet deep, not as large as most people think—humble yet glorious, like Jesus. On top of the ark was a thick slab of gold that served as a lid. This was called the mercy seat, because here the high priest sprinkled the sacrificial blood representing the atoning blood of Jesus.

The Israelites didn't fully understand the Messianic implications of the ark, but they knew it represented the presence of God going before them as a vanguard. The ark was carried by priests who bore it on poles. Joshua commanded the people to follow three-quarters of a mile behind the ark so everyone could see it. If the masses had crowded around it, almost no one could have seen it.

As David M. Howard, Jr., wrote, "These two aspects of God's nature—his close, comforting presence and his awesome, fearsome glory—are kept in a healthy balance in the Bible."[13]

Even so, the presence of the Lord—both grace-filled and

glorious—goes three-quarters of a mile before you into the next stage of life. In other words, He is three-quarters of an hour ahead of you. Three-quarters of a month ahead of you. Three-quarters of a year ahead of you. Three-quarters of a lifetime ahead of you. Your Lord is already in your future, clearing the way, arranging the circumstances in advance, and preparing the work you'll do, the burdens you'll bear, and the blessings you'll enjoy.

Furthermore, the ark wasn't an empty chest. It contained three items—the rod of Aaron that had budded (representing God's power); the tablets of the Ten Commandments (representing God's precepts); and a jar of heavenly manna (representing God's provision).

Think of it!

You don't know what the future holds—not even tomorrow. You are heading where you've never been before. But Jesus goes before you with His power, His precepts, and His provisions—all you need to make the most of tomorrow's sunshine or shadows.

And so the Israelites broke camp at the Acacia Grove, folded their tents, packed their donkeys, gathered their children, and traveled ten miles to the banks of the Jordan River, which was at flood stage and impassable for such a multitude. They could only expect that God had a plan to lead them to a place—and in a way—they had never been before.

He did.

READ THE COMPASS

Unbelief says, "Let's go back to where it's safe," but faith says, "Let's go forward to where God is working."

—WARREN W. WIERSBE

If I didn't believe God had a plan for my life and was leading me step by step, I'd sink in the quagmire. From childhood I grew up singing, "Savior, like a Shepherd, lead me," and no biblical truth has sustained my spirits more than the assurance of God's guidance. Psalm 37:23 says, "A person's steps are established by the LORD, and he takes pleasure in his way." In other words, the Lord not only establishes our steps in advance, He is delighted when we follow the pathway He has ordained. He leads us where we've never been before.

In practical terms, how do God's will and our decision-making merge into a strategic system? Let's view it as a soldier's compass.

At the center, it begins with a deep conviction of God's sovereignty—His utter, eternal jurisdiction over every detail of the past, present, and future, from the farthest stars in His galaxies to the deepest scars of His children. He guides because He governs. He makes a way for us because nothing can stop Him. He is ascendant over every despot and dominant over every detail. He oversees everything; He overlooks nothing—not the mysteries of His cosmos or the miseries of His children. His redemptive power turns every curse into a blessing for those who love Him and seek His will. Most of our worries would instantly vanish if we grasped the extremity of God's sovereignty.

The circumference of the compass is wholehearted willingness. The Lord doesn't lead those who won't follow, and our own stubborn self-will can ruin His plans for us. The Lord says, "I will instruct you and show you the way to go; with my eye on you, I will give counsel. Do not be like a horse or mule" (Psalm 32:8-9). We have to say, as the Israelites did in Joshua 1:16, "Everything you have commanded us we will do, and everywhere you send us we will go."

Now let's look at the face of the compass and its four points—NSEW.

The N stands for Nearness. The most critical element of guidance is remaining close to the Shepherd as He leads us. The Israelites had to stay three-quarters of a mile back, but we have the privilege of being as close to Him as we wish—and the closer the better. The psalmist said, "Yet I am always with you; you hold my right hand. You guide me with your counsel, and afterward you will take me up in glory…. God's presence is my good" (Psalm 73:23-24, 28).

The S on the dial stands for Scripture. You'll not find a verse that says, "Enroll in Harvard," or, "Buy a Ford." But as you spend time reading and meditating on Scripture day and night (as Joshua 1:8 commands), you'll begin to gain divine wisdom in human affairs, and you'll find biblical truths that shine light upon your path and enlighten your thinking.

The E stands for Events and clarifying circumstances. When Katrina and I were married in 1976, I expected to begin pastoring a church at once—but no job offers came. We spent a full year living near my parents. I worked at JCPenney, and we made our home in a Presbyterian manse, offered rent-free if I preached at the church once a month. I couldn't have planned a better first year of marriage. I learned to be a husband and preacher (and to sell shoes), and Katrina learned to be a wife and homemaker (and store clerk). We had to follow the circumstances, but God was in the details of them.

The W represents Weighing the options. Proverbs 16:9 says, "A person's heart plans his way, but the Lord determines his steps." The Lord expects us to use our hearts and minds to think through decisions and make wise plans. In the process, He guides us and determines our steps.

The psalmist said, "Make your ways known to me, Lord; teach me your paths. Guide me in your truth and teach me, for…I wait for you all day long" (Psalm 25:4-5).

God is ready to lead you where you've never been before. The prospect may seem threatening, but consider this scene from *The Pilgrim's Progress*. As Mr. Christian pursued his journey from the City of Destruction to the Celestial City, he heard reports of two fierce lions in the pathway ahead. He trembled and hesitated to proceed.

Mr. Watchful noticed Christian's faltering steps and cried to him, "Is your strength and courage so small? Why are you afraid? Do you still have no faith? Don't be afraid of the lions for they are chained. They are placed there to test your faith at this point in the journey. So stay in the middle of the path and you will not be harmed."

Still trembling, Christian edged his way forward. The lions strained at their chains, roaring and snarling, but they couldn't touch him as long as he stayed in the middle of the road. Christian clapped his hands with joy and went on his way.[14]

Even if you hear the roaring of lions, don't be afraid. Stay in the middle of the path and go onward! Remember…

> Deep in unfathomable mines
> Of never-failing skill,

[God] treasures up His bright designs
And works His sovereign will.

WILLIAM COWPER

For individual and group study materials, including videos and study guides, and for discounts on bulk purchases, visit jordanriverrules.com

JORDAN RIVER RULE #6

PREPARE TODAY FOR TOMORROW'S WONDERS

JOSHUA 3:5-8

Joshua told the people, "Consecrate yourselves, because the Lord will do wonders among you tomorrow."

—JOSHUA 3:5

CONSECRATE YOURSELF

Half-heartedness spoils the sacrifice. Postponement is peril-
ous.... Consecrate, consecrate yourselves, body and soul and
spirit, to God now.

—J. B. LIGHTFOOT

While waiting in a grocery line, do you ever pick up a tab-
loid and see a story about some young prince from a royal
family who causes endless problems for his father, the king,
or his mother, the queen? You know the type. A young man,
born in the palace, destined for the crown, representing a
kingdom. Yet here he is causing scandals, sowing wild oats,
and living the life of the prodigal son.

What's his problem?

His condition doesn't match his position.

Before we shake our heads in disdain, let's remember, as
Christ-followers, we're children of the King representing
a royal family and a Kingdom. Heaven doesn't have tab-
loids; but if it did, would the angels be reading about you

and me and shaking their heads because our habits don't match our calling?

After the Israelites had traveled the final ten miles of their wilderness journey from the Acacia Grove to the swollen Jordan, Joshua sent this message through the ranks: "Consecrate yourselves, because the Lord will do wonders among you tomorrow" (Joshua 3:5).

That's a sentence to engrave on a plaque and hang in your home or office. But what does it mean? The word *consecrate* and its frequent New Testament synonym *sanctify* convey the idea of holiness, of being set apart for sacred use. According to Exodus 19:9-15, this involved ritual purification for the Jewish soldiers.

The rituals represented a spiritual reality. A holy God needs holy people if He's going to do great things among them. Sanctity, consecration, and personal holiness are essential if our Lord is going to do wonders through us. We need our condition to reflect our position. But how does that happen?

OUR POSITION

It clearly begins when we definitively receive Jesus Christ as our Lord and Savior, for only He can truly make us holy. The apostle Paul wrote to the Corinthians—a flawed church—and told them: "No sexually immoral people, idolaters, adulterers, or males who have sex with males, no thieves, greedy people, drunkards, verbally abusive people, or swindlers will inherit God's kingdom. And some of you used to be like this. But you were washed, you were sanctified, you were justified in the name of the Lord Jesus Christ and by the Spirit of our God" (1 Corinthians 6:9-11).

The city of Corinth was an overflowing sewer of evil, but God had washed and sanctified and justified those who had come to Christ by the power of the Holy Spirit. He had declared them holy in His sight. They weren't yet perfect in terms of their condition, but they were holy in their position in Christ. Hebrews 13:12 says, "Therefore, Jesus also suffered outside the gate, so that he might sanctify the people by his own blood."

Consecrating ourselves, then, begins by committing our lives to Jesus Christ and to the power of His blood, which is able to wash away our sins and make us holy in God's sight—as holy as if we had never sinned.

OUR CONDITION

If that's our position in Christ, then our part in the process is to grow in Jesus so our condition increasingly matches our position. Ephesians 4:1 tells us "to walk worthy of the calling [we] have received."

The Bible says, "For just as you offered the parts of yourselves as slaves to impurity, and to greater and greater lawlessness, so now offer them as slaves to righteousness, which results in sanctification" (Romans 6:19).

The apostle Paul told us "to take off [our] former way of life, the old self that is corrupted by deceitful desires, to be renewed in the spirit of [our] minds, and to put on the new self, the one created according to God's likeness in righteousness and purity of the truth" (Ephesians 4:22-24).

Is a bad habit in your life hindering the work of Christ?

Is a good habit missing due to carelessness?

Is the gap between your position and your condition growing wider or slimmer?

Is your daily walk with Christ becoming stronger or weaker?

My father owned and operated Sunset Orchard in the mountains of North Carolina. He loved apple blossom season when the trees turned into masses of white and pink; then he carefully tended the crop as the tiny apples emerged and began to grow. But apples are more delicate than they appear and are susceptible to various molds, fungi, viruses, and insects. Blight can spread through a tree quickly. When one apple begins to rot, the decay spreads very rapidly to every apple it touches. My dad did his best to check every apple on every tree; and at the first sign something was amiss, he went to work—destroying the bad apple and spraying the others.

If something is amiss in your life, be proactive. Repent.

Change. Ask God for help in overcoming the temptation and ridding yourself of the rot. Take Joshua 3:5 seriously and work on it every day: Consecrate yourself, because the Lord will do wonders through you tomorrow.

> Now may the God of peace himself sanctify you completely (some translations say "through and through"). And may your whole spirit, soul, and body be kept sound and blameless at the coming of our Lord Jesus Christ. (1 Thessalonians 5:23)

THE LORD WILL DO WONDERS
AMONG YOU TOMORROW

I labor for this, striving with his strength that works power-fully in me.

—COLOSSIANS 1:29

The promise is clear. If we consecrate ourselves, the Lord will do wonders among us. He will bless us, and He will use us more than we realize.

My friend David Ra, the director of a large Asian ministry, told me of meeting a Christian brother named Koko who had been born in Myanmar but moved to New York City with his family as a youngster. Koko excelled in school. After graduating, he became a high commissioner at the United Nations, and his area of specialty was Myanmar.

Koko was deeply concerned that the government of his native land made it difficult to share the Gospel. Every religious gathering was reported to the government and many meetings were not allowed at all. "The most urgent thing in my country is to have an open door policy," Koko said. "I need to specifically pray for this."

Koko contacted major church leaders in Myanmar and asked, "Are you praying that the government implement an open door policy?" Many were not due to discouragement. He then contacted Myanmar church leaders in the United States, and many of them agreed to join in intercessory prayer.

Years passed, and the situation seemed to worsen. Many praying churches lost heart and stopped praying. But Koko refused to lose heart. He and a few determined friends prayed without stopping.

Then one day, to everyone's surprise, the military regime of Myanmar released a major democratic advocate from house arrest and guaranteed safe passage for anti-government figures who were staying overseas. This new open door policy took the world by surprise. It's almost unknown for a tight military regime to change course. Overseas investors swarmed into Myanmar, and the streets were filled with waves of freedom.

In 2013, the United States government invited Myanmar's president and cabinet officials to America for the first time in forty-seven years. The delegation visited New York and conducted an official press conference. As it turned out, Koko was the official interpreter.

The biggest single question at the press conference was, "Why did Myanmar change its political philosophy and reform its policy?"

President Thein Sein smiled but didn't answer.

"Was it because of UN's resolutions?" asked a reporter.

"Was it because of EU and US economic sanctions?"

Finally, Mr. Thein Sein opened his mouth and answered, saying, "No, we felt no heavy blow of economic sanctions because we had China's help. And the United Nations just issues resolutions but takes no actions, so it was like a paper tiger to us. We were not afraid of it at all."

"Then what was the real reason you implemented an open door and reformation policy?"

With a short moment of silence, the president replied, "It was because of Phantom."

"What is Phantom?" asked the journalists.

The president said, "Some years ago, a phantom appeared to several strongmen of my country and threatened to kill them if they did not accept an open door and reformation policy. This lasted several years. Finally, those threatened by the phantom gathered, discussed it, and decided to accept an open door and reformation policy. They thought it would be better than being killed by a phantom."

When Koko returned home, he was exhausted but went to prayer. He himself was puzzled by the president's strange answer. But as he prayed, he seemed to realize perhaps the strange phantom was actually the Holy Spirit. To those non-believing strongmen, the Holy Spirit would have felt like a phantom.

When I visited Myanmar, I was amazed at the vibrant Christian community and the growth of the church.

I spoke to a huge congregation, which included the vice president of Myanmar and his family. Christians who worshiped underground for years are now building wonderful churches and spreading the Gospel at home and abroad. Even though recent events have demonstrated the instability of the politics of Myanmar, as we continue to pray, I'm convinced the Gospel will continue to grow in that beautiful nation.

Don't underestimate how God can use you and your prayers. The New King James Version of Daniel 11:32 says, "The people who know their God shall be strong, and carry out great exploits."

Consecrate yourself today, and let God use you as He will tomorrow.

For individual and group study materials, including videos and study guides, and for discounts on bulk purchases, visit jordanriverrules.com

Jordan River Rule #7

Trust God to Turn Problems Into Pathways

Joshua 3:9-17

Now the Jordan overflows its banks throughout the harvest season. But as soon as the priests carrying the ark reached the Jordan, their feet touched the water at its edge and the water flowing downstream stood still, rising up in a mass.... and the people crossed opposite Jericho.... all Israel crossed on dry ground until the entire nation had finished crossing the Jordan.

—Joshua 3:15-17

On Jordan's Stormy Banks

He turned the sea into dry land,
And they crossed the river on foot.
There we rejoiced in him.

—Psalm 66:6

The first time I saw the Jordan River, I was underwhelmed. It was in 1976 on my first visit to Israel, and it was a small, green river, about the size of the river that flowed beside my house in Elizabethton, Tennessee. The Jordan used to be much larger. Massive irrigation on both sides of the river has reduced its size. One source reports the Jordan River is now only about three percent of what it was about one hundred years ago.[15]

An 1854 book describes the Jordan as being one hundred feet across at Jericho, with a depth of ten to twenty feet. The stream was too swift for swimmers.[16] I've seen a 1935 picture of the Jordan at flood stage. The melting snows of Mount Hermon rush down the Jordan Valley and turn the gentle river into a deluge that soaks the ground on both banks. As the floods receded, I'm told, farmers would cast their seed upon the waters and, in this way, plant their crops. That's the possible meaning of Ecclesiastes 11:1: "Send your bread (seed) on the surface of the water, for after many days you may find it."

We have to admire the faith of the Israelites. At God's command, they loaded up their families and belongings and marched undauntedly toward this angry river, preceded by priests bearing the ark of the covenant. Joshua 3:15-17 says:

> As soon as the priests carrying the ark reached the Jordan, their feet touched the water at its edge and the water flowing downstream stood still, rising up in a mass.... The water flowing downstream into the Sea of the Arabah—the Dead Sea—was completely cut off, and the people crossed opposite Jericho. The priests carrying the ark of the Lord's covenant stood firmly on dry ground in the middle of the Jordan, while all Israel crossed on dry ground until the entire nation had finished crossing the Jordan.

It's as though an invisible glass barrier—a divine dam—fell across the river. The waters parted, the ground solidified, and the thousands of Israelites passed over dry shod, just as their parents had marched through the Red Sea forty years earlier. The same God who led them out was leading them on. The living God was among them (Joshua 3:10)!

Interestingly, the prophets Elijah and Elisha later performed the same miracle near the same spot in 2 Kings 2. Centuries later, at roughly the same place, the Lord Jesus Christ descended into the Jordan and was baptized. This time it wasn't the waters that parted but the heavens, as the Holy Spirit descended like a dove and anointed Him with power for His earthly ministry.

What a sacred spot! And what a lesson for us! God knows how to turn problems into pathways and barriers into breakthroughs. If He says, "Go forward," then take the next steps by faith. He intends to provide an opening through every obstacle, and His sovereign power can do exceedingly abundantly more than we can ask or imagine.

For years, engineers dreamed of constructing a canal across Panama to connect the Atlantic and Pacific Oceans. The Americans tackled the project in 1904 and finished the job ten years later—an amazing engineering feat. During the venture, the workers maintained their morale with this song.

> Got any river they say is uncrossable?
> Got any mountains that can't be cut through?
> We specialize in the wholly impossible,
> Doing things nobody ever could do.[17]

In 1942, Pastor Oscar Carl Eliason, a Swedish-American evangelist and hymnist, turned those lyrics into a gospel song based on the parting of the Jordan River:

> *Got any rivers you think are uncrossable?*
> *Got any mountains you can't tunnel through?*
> *God specializes in things thought impossible—*
> *He does the things others cannot do.*[18]

Do you have any rivers you think are uncrossable? Ask God to turn your problems into pathways, then trust Him to part the waters as you press forward into the future. He does things others cannot do. He can divide the waters.

Or He might have something else in mind....

WHAT IF THE RIVER
DOESN'T PART?

---

*Many pilgrims passing through these Red Seas and Jordans
of affliction will be enabled in the retrospect of eternity to
say, "We went through the flood on foot, there did we rejoice
in Him."*[19]

—JOHN ROSS MACDUFF

The Lord doesn't always do as we expect. If you come to
the water's edge and the waters don't part, I have another
passage for you—Isaiah 43:1-2:

I have called you by your name; you are mine.
When you pass through the waters, I will be with you,
And the rivers will not overwhelm you.

Some years ago, *Backpacker Magazine* ran an article on
how to ford a river. The writer warned that river and stream
crossings can be the most dangerous part of backpacking,

and river drownings cause more hiking deaths than snake-bites. "The best way to cross a river is with a rope as a safe-guard," said the magazine. If you have a group of hikers, the strongest should wade into the river with ropes under his armpits connected to hikers upstream and downstream. Once on the other side, he should secure the ropes to a strong tree using a carabiner and sling; and the others can then cross one by one, secured by the suspended rope.[20]

Our Lord Jesus has already crossed the river of every challenge we'll ever face, and He has secured the rope of grace to the tree of God's omnipotence. We simply hold on by faith and proceed one step at a time. Isaiah 43:2 is a great verse to grip.

In November 1997, Vianne Nichols, who was in her fifties, was grieving her husband's death when she was diagnosed with breast cancer. The shock overwhelmed her. But for years, she'd had a magnet on her refrigerator with the words of Isaiah 43:2: *When you pass through the waters, I will be with you, and the rivers will not overwhelm you.* She claimed that verse as her own, and it became a rope that guided her through the torrent. "During and after cancer treatment, I often read the scripture with a grateful heart and new insight," she said.

She's now been a cancer survivor for more than twenty years.[21]

Jonah Meshell is a boy in Cassville, Missouri, who loves

Jesus and karate. He began karate lessons at age four, and by the time he was nine he was competing. Along the way, he was diagnosed with ADHD, which at first embarrassed him. But he had a belt made for his karate outfit. The belt was orange, and it was engraved with his favorite Bible verse—Isaiah 43:2. He's pressing on. He sometimes imagines being a Hollywood stuntman and using his career to share the message of Jesus.[22]

And then there's Charles Towne, who put Isaiah 43:2 into practice literally. He grew up beside the Fox River in Oswego, Illinois. It occasionally flooded; and once, the flood washed away the family's boat, leaving them marooned. All night Charles heard the waters on either side of the house, with the sounds of the debris charging downstream. The next day, Charles decided to swim to the mainland. As best he can remember, he had a hot date. Wrapping his clothes in a piece of oiled canvas, and wearing a pair of cut-offs, he launched into the flood.

Charles badly underestimated the force of the river, and he struggled to stay above water as trees and branches swept by him. A dead cow, spinning in the current, floated past and seemed to grin maliciously at him. He had repeated encounters with near drowning.

"I swam and finally, what seemed like hours later, almost at the limit of my extremity, my feet finally touched bottom, and I staggered from the river's deadly embrace."

He was terrified, exhausted, and a quarter-mile downstream.

Whenever he remembers that day, he thinks of Isaiah 43:2, and his prayer is: "As the waters of life at times seem about to overwhelm me, you have always carried me to safety.... Walk with me now oh Lord, and buoy me up.... In Jesus' holy and beautiful name I ask this, Amen."[23]

The writer of "How Firm a Foundation" marvelously paraphrased Isaiah 43:2 in his great hymn. In my opinion, this is one of the most poignant stanzas ever penned, and I often share it with those in difficult spots. Perhaps it will encourage you today.

When through the deep waters I call thee to go,
The rivers of sorrow shall not overflow,
For I will be with thee, thy troubles to bless
And sanctify to thee thy deepest distress.

What if You Fall
Into the River?

---

*He reached down from on high and took hold of me; he pulled
me out of deep water.*

—Psalm 18:16

Several years ago, I spent a week with my friend Bark
Fahnestock, who had worked in Ethiopia in dangerous
times. He gave me a book entitled *Warriors of Ethiopia,*
written by his coworker, and one of the stories illustrates
how God can turn troubling rivers into glorious gains.

A national Ethiopian evangelist named Laliso wanted
to take the Gospel to Goybi village. He intended to reach
the village before sunset but was delayed at a police check-
point. At nightfall, Laliso was still on the dangerous trail.
As best he could, he followed a narrow path through the
dark forest. The edge of the pathway formed a steep slope
with a river down below.

Suddenly the pathway gave way, causing Laliso to tum-
ble down the bank and splash into the river, scratched and

soaked to the skin. The banks were too steep to climb, so Laliso had to slog upstream, looking for a place to exit the chilling current.

By and by he saw a level spot and called out for help. He heard approaching voices, and he asked if he was near Goybi. A small group told him he had arrived at the village and helped him onto solid ground.

A man holding a light said, "He is the fair one and he came to us out of the water!" A mummer of excitement arose. An older man asked, "But does he have them? Has he brought the golden leaves?"

The villagers took Laliso to a hut where he wrung out his clothes and had a bite of supper. More people crowded into the house. These people had dark skin, and Laliso's was lighter. He wondered why the people were so excited a fair-skinned man had come out of the river. Then a local village medicine man arrived and stared at Laliso for some time. Pressing his hands together and opening them, as if shutting and opening a book, he kept repeating, "The leaves. The gold leaves."

Laliso prayed for guidance, then unwrapped his Bible. It had a black cover but the edges of the pages were gold. The people gasped. "It is true! The gold leaves have come!" they said. The medicine man explained, "A long time ago, before my father died, he told us that one day a fair man would come to us out of the water with some gold leaves.

The gold leaves were the truth to show us the way of life. We have waited for the truth for so long. But now you have come."

Laliso began preaching the Gospel, and dozens of people accepted Christ. The work continues today as the Good News spreads through that corner of the world.[24]

Sometimes God doesn't part the river. He allows us to fall into it. But He has a preordained plan, and if we persevere—even against the flow—He will be glorified and the Gospel will spread. The way forward is by faith, with the Holy Spirit within us and the golden leaves in our hands and in our heart.

Whatever happens with your Jordan, never forget to trust your Jesus.

For individual and group study materials, including videos and study guides, and for discounts on bulk purchases, visit jordanriverrules.com

Jordan River Rule #8

Build a Monument

Joshua 4

Then Joshua set up in Gilgal the twelve stones they had taken from the Jordan, and he said to the Israelites, "In the future, when your children ask their fathers, 'What is the meaning of these stones?' you should tell your children, 'Israel crossed the Jordan on dry ground.'"

—Joshua 4:20-22

Monumental Moments

---

*Their departure from Egypt and their arrival in Canaan
are signalized by parallel miracles of sea and river. Both at
their exit and at their entrance Jehovah leads them through
a watery gate, by cleaving the waves asunder.*

—Dr. D. Steele

As the priests stood in the middle of the riverbed securing the poles of the ark of the covenant, hundreds of thousands of people hurried across, led by forty thousand soldiers in battle formation from the three Transjordan tribes. After the final straggler reached the western bank, Joshua sent twelve Israeli ironmen back to where the priests were standing. Each of the warriors pried up a huge stone, hoisted it onto his shoulder, and brought it to Joshua. The priests followed the strong men out of the riverbed, and the foaming waters surged through the ravine.

The Children of Israel were finally in the Promised Land. Their feet were on Canaan's soil—and there was no going back. The Jordan, which had enabled their entrance, now blocked their retreat. And the twelve large stones?

Then Joshua set up in Gilgal the twelve stones they had taken from the Jordan, and he said to the Israelites, "In the future, when your children ask their fathers, 'What is the meaning of these stones?' you should tell your children, 'Israel crossed the Jordan on dry ground.' For the Lord your God dried up the water of the Jordan before you until you had crossed over, just as the Lord your God did to the Red Sea, which he dried up before us until we had crossed over. This is so that all the peoples of the earth may know that the Lord's hand is strong, and so that you may always fear the Lord your God." (Joshua 4:20-24)

When I look back over my seven decades, I realize I could never have charted my own path or understood the end from the beginning. Only God knew the way through the wilderness. He has parted waters, sustained me in many rivers, and sometimes pulled me out of the depths. My story is unlike anyone else's in history—and so is yours. It's amazing. Our God has a unique pathway for each one of His billions of followers; and the further we progress with Him, the more we praise Him for leading us in righteous paths.

Someone else should know what Christ has done in your life. Why not take some of the stones of your experience and build a monument? Your children, grandchildren, nieces, nephews, or friends should know your story and how God led you, blessed you, and used you. You should leave a testimony behind—an Ebenezer.

In 1 Samuel 7, God gave the Israelites a tremendous victory over their archenemies, the Philistines. "Afterward, Samuel took a stone and set it upright between Mizpah and Shen. He named it Ebenezer, explaining, 'The Lord has helped us to this point'" (1 Samuel 7:12).

The word *Ebenezer* means "stone of help." It was a monument to future generations that hitherto the Lord had helped them. Likewise, Psalm 71:18 says, "Even while I am old and gray, God, do not abandon me, while I proclaim your power to another generation, your strength to all who are to come."

Our greatest ministry will occur after we're dead—that is, after we're in heaven. We'll leave behind all the work we've done, the tasks we've completed, the words we've said and written, the people we've touched, the causes we've supported, the lives we've changed, the children we've raised, the churches we've sustained, the missionaries we've sent, and the funds we've invested in the Kingdom. It all has a ripple effect that expands until Christ returns.

"Blessed are the dead who die in the Lord…. they will rest from their labors, since their works follow them" (Revelation 14:13).

When Martin Luther unleashed the Reformation in 1517, there followed a surge of enthusiasm that transformed the German church. But as the years passed, the Lutheran church lost its steam. Then came the Thirty Years'

War. As the war was winding down, a baby was born in Germany, Philipp Spener, who later helped unleash the great Lutheran revival known as Pietism.

Spener had a profound influence on an eager young man named August Hermann Francke. In 1695, Francke opened his home to poor children to receive schooling in Halle, Germany. By his death in 1727, more than 2,000 children were receiving care and instruction from 170 teachers.

A hundred years later, in 1826, a German university student named George Müller enrolled at Halle University and took up lodgings in Francke's orphanage, and he was deeply moved by the work he saw. Seven years later, Müller was moved by the Holy Spirit to establish a similar ministry to homeless children in Bristol, England, and the story of Müller's life became a classic of Christian history.

A few years ago, my daughter, Victoria, and her family read the story of George Müller and were inspired to adopt two children from a violent home. I now have two wonderful grandchildren because of a chain of events going back to Martin Luther in 1517—more than five hundred years ago.

The Almighty has a unique plan for each of us that involves leaving a legacy with an echo chamber that will reverberate until Christ returns. Don't underestimate how the next stage of your life will influence generations yet unborn. Find a way to preserve a testimony.

It can be monumental.

PEBBLES IN THE PATHWAY

A river reaches places which its source never knows.... God rarely allows a person to see how great a blessing he is to others.

—OSWALD CHAMBERS

Most of us aren't going to leave physical monuments comprised of boulders, but we can pick up some pebbles in the pathway and arrange them as a spiritual inheritance for those who come behind us. How? I can think of many ways; I'll mention three.

First, write your testimony, your story, and an account of your life. How I wish my parents and grandparents had done this! You can have it self-published, or you can simply leave a few copies—handwritten or typed—in your desk drawer or lockbox. You can post it online in ways that will preserve its contents.

It's easier than you think. Take an hour one night to list the important dates and events of your life—your birth, your baptism, the process of how you came to Christ, your wedding, your first job, your second job, your military service, the births of your children, your medical emergency, your moments of crisis, your retirement—whatever it is. Jot down anything that seems significant to you. Develop a personal chronology of your life.

In the coming days, weeks, or months, begin filling in some of the details. Don't try to create a literary masterpiece. Just write a simple autobiography as if you were telling your life's story to a friend. Make sure to include the ways God led you, blessed you, helped you, and used you.

In his manuscript *Ink: Your Story and the Power of the Pen,* my friend Dr. Kevin Moore wrote: "What an incredible gift to be able to give your children! My books are a window into my soul. Even long after I am gone, my children will be able to read my books and grow in their faith. If God can use my books to help disciple my children, then it will make all of the countless hours worthwhile. Your book can impact people you will never meet in places you have never been. And long after you are gone, your written words may continue to make a powerful impact for the Lord Jesus Christ."[25]

Second, we can leave behind a personal Bible. My friend Ida Lewis told me, "My mother left me the best of what she had when she went to heaven. I have her Bible! It was used in her ministry to others for many, many years and is filled with notes made on the pages of many of her talks and lessons. What a sweet treasure to me."

For my own daily devotions, I use a wide margin Bible and an engineer's pencil. I hope one day the pages of personal notes will encourage some chip-off-the-block whom I'll not meet until heaven. My friend Dr. David Outlaw has purposefully done this for each of his five children, using different Bibles.

Third, we leave monuments by what we do with our lives and by what we give. I love visiting the Word of Life campground in the Adirondacks, where each year hundreds of young people make decisions for Christ. My friend Larry Bollback told me of a man who visited one night. As he crossed to the island, the man said, almost to himself, "This is about all that I have left."

That night about two hundred teenagers came forward at the campfire service. As the man was leaving and returning to the mainland, a friend asked him about his earlier statement. "When we got here this evening you looked around and said, 'This is about all I have left.' What did you mean by that?"

The man explained that at one time he was owner of a large trucking company with a fleet of two hundred trucks, and he gave a very large contribution to Word of Life to make possible the purchase of that island. Since that time, the man's company had experienced a significant downturn, and he was down to one truck. His investment in the island was about all he had left.

His friend looked at him and reminded him that two hundred young people had made decisions in that one service; there had been multiple campfire services all over the Word of Life properties that evening, and he could multiply that by all the weeks of the summer and by all the years the camp had been in existence—more than seventy years now.

"If this is all you left," said the friend, "you are a very rich man."[26]

Live faithfully, give freely, make notes in your Bible, write some things down, and leave some footprints. Pick up some pebbles in the pathway, which God will transform into pearls of great price for those who come behind you. You'll be leaving behind a legacy richer than you know—a monument of mercy and a pillar of praise.

For individual and group study materials, including videos and study guides, and for discounts on bulk purchases, visit jordanriverrules.com

JORDAN RIVER RULE #9

YOU'RE NOT IN CHARGE, BUT REMEMBER WHO IS

JOSHUA 5:13–6:5

When Joshua was near Jericho, he looked up and saw a man standing in front of him with a drawn sword in his hand.

—JOSHUA 5:13

The Commander of the Lord's Army

Did we in our own strength confide, our striving would be losing; Were not the right Man on our side, the Man of God's own choosing.

—Martin Luther

Leaving the river behind them, the Israelites marched toward the great city of Jericho, their first major roadblock into the Promised Land. Word of their presence spread through the Canaanite canyons and hills, and every town and village was tense with dread.

When all the Amorite kings across the Jordan to the west and all the Canaanite kings near the sea heard how the Lord had dried up the water of the Jordan before the Israelites until they had crossed over, they lost heart and their courage failed. (Joshua 5:1)

In Joshua 5, the Israelites set up camp at Gilgal, reestablished the Jewish rite of circumcision, then observed the Passover. They reenacted the moment from forty years earlier when their parents had killed the Passover lambs, painted the doorposts of their slave huts, and prepared to leave Egypt.

Then Joshua turned his attention to Jericho, which was "strongly fortified because of the Israelites—no one leaving or entering" (Joshua 6:1). Joshua didn't have a clue how to conquer the city. The walls were impenetrable, and because Jericho was an oasis in the desert, its inhabitants had plenty of food and water.

Do you have any obstacles blocking your path, with no clue how to conquer them? To the Israelites, Jericho was a literal roadblock. We have lots of those as we move through life, one stage at a time. Limitations. Hindrances. Hurdles. Obstacles. Or you might have another word for it—handicap, impoverishment, disease, depression, foreclosure, unfaithfulness, unemployment, loneliness, grief, addiction.

Joshua simply called it *Jericho*, and he had no idea what to do next. As he scrutinized the situation, he was startled to see an imposing soldier with a drawn sword, perhaps twenty feet away. The two warriors sized each other up, and finally Joshua ventured closer and demanded, "Are you for us or for our enemies?"

"Neither," he replied. "I have now come as commander of the Lord's army."

Then Joshua bowed with his face to the ground in worship and asked him, "What does my lord want to say to his servant?" (See Joshua 5:13-14)

This was no angel, not even an archangel. This was the Lord Sabaoth—the Lord of hosts, the enigmatic figure known as the Angel or Messenger of the Lord, whom we understand to have been the preincarnate (pre-Bethlehem) Lord Jesus Christ Himself.

This Commander is invincible, and His command extends to the edges of the universe and beyond. Behind Him in the unseen realms are millions of angelic troops— the hosts of heaven—ready to implement God's plan—in this case, to provide a homeland to Abraham's descendants.

What a moment! Joshua came face to face with *Yeshua*.

The Commander of the Lord's hosts held a drawn sword, indicating the judgment that was about to descend on the Canaanite tribes who had been stewing in their wickedness for four hundred years.

The commander of the Lord's army said to Joshua, "Remove the sandals from your feet, for the place where you are standing is holy." And Joshua did that. (Joshua 5:15)

Why this command?

Look at it again: This is holy ground, so take off your shoes.

When we are standing upright, the soles of our feet are the only parts of our body to touch the ground. Doctors tell us we have as many as 200,000 nerve endings in each sole, and the weight of our entire bodies rests on them. The nerves travel unusually fast from our feet to our brains—it's a neurological expressway. By taking off his shoes, Joshua was actually touching ground supremely holy with nothing to get in the way of the experience.

The ground within a certain circumference of our Lord's physical presence became radioactive with righteousness and cauterized with holiness. Those grains of sand became as holy as the soil of heaven itself, as pure as the golden streets of New Jerusalem.

How better to experience it than directly—with bare feet! Who would want to miss that experience? When Joshua removed his shoes, his entire two-hundred-or-so pounds tangibly sunk into hot and holy earth.

If the very ground is holy, you don't want anything between it and you. You want to feel the holiness from the soles of your feet to the depths of your soul. You want to experience the sacredness of holy ground as its precious dust covers your feet and as your toes sink into its sand.

That doesn't mean, I suppose, we should literally take off our shoes whenever we have a problem. But here's what it does mean: Whenever you have an obstacle you cannot overcome, you're standing on holy ground. The Lord is unusually near. He descends to deliver. He arrives with a plan, which will be unlike anything you imagined, and it's a special opportunity to experience His holy and blessed presence.

Stop obsessing over your Jericho and look to your *Iesous,* your Jesus.

He knows exactly what to do next.

> *You ask who that may be?*
> *Christ Jesus, it is He;*
> *Lord Sabaoth His name*
> *From age to age the same;*
> *And He must win the battle.*

— A MIGHTY FORTRESS IS OUR GOD

RUNNING CIRCLES
AROUND THE ENEMY

---

*Those walls fell down because smitten by the impact of
celestial hosts.*

—DR. F. B. MEYER

An old commentary on the book of Joshua said, "There
is no more unfortunate division of chapters in the Bible
than occurs here. The conversation between the Captain
and his lieutenant is cut in twain."[27]

When we read through the book of Joshua, most of us
stop at the end of chapter 5, thinking the story of the
Commander of the Lord's host abruptly ends. Actually, it
continues into chapter 6 as the Commander proceeds to
give Joshua the plan for conquering Jericho.

Lord Sabaoth goes on to say:

Look, I have handed Jericho, its king, and its best soldiers over to you. March around the city with all the
men of war, circling the city one time. Do this for six

days. Have seven priests carry seven ram's-horn trumpets in front of the ark. But on the seventh day, march around the city seven times, while the priests blow the ram's horns. When there is a prolonged blast of the horn and you hear its sound, have all the troops give a mighty shout. Then the city wall will collapse, and the troops will advance, each man straight ahead. (Joshua 6:2-5)

This is the oddest military strategy ever given to a general by his commander in the history of warfare.

Or is it?

It reminds me of how God used Gideon's three hundred men with torches and pitchers to rout the Midianites (Judges 7); how He used David's slingshot to rout the Philistines (1 Samuel 17); how He used Jehoshaphat's temple choir to defeat the invading hordes in 2 Chronicles 20; how He sent a single angel to slay 185,000 soldiers in Hezekiah's time (2 Chronicles 32 and 2 Kings 19); and how a small band of ordinary and uneducated men turned the world upside down in New Testament days (Acts 4:13 and 17:6).

The Bible says, "Now we have this treasure in clay jars, so that this extraordinary power may be from God and not from us" (2 Corinthians 4:7). We're cracked pots, but we're not shrinking violets. We're ready to go where He leads and do whatever He tells us. But whatever is done, He's the one who will do it.

Isaiah 26:12 says, "Lord,… you have also done all our work for us."

In other words, whatever we achieve is simply the result of what God Himself does. He accomplishes our achievements for us. Everything we think we're doing is truly His doing. He is doing it in, for, through, and around us; and the life we now live in the flesh, we live through faith in the Son of God who loved us and gave Himself for us.

If you're bearing the strain of a load too heavy, a pain too hurtful, a project too big, or an obstacle too rigid, remember you're not in charge. Your moments of greatest perplexity are His moments to show up as the Commander of the Lord's hosts. You're on holy ground.

Take some time worshiping Him and basking in the power of God's encircling holiness.

And so it was that the people who had marched around in circles for decades were about to march in more circles—for seven days.

They were about to run—or rather, walk—circles around their foes.

For individual and group study materials, including videos and study guides, and for discounts on bulk purchases, visit jordanriverrules.com

Jordan River Rule #10

Encircle Obstacles With Biblical Faith and Shout the Victory

Joshua 6

The priests took the ark of the Lord, and the seven priests carrying seven ram's horns marched in front of the ark of the Lord. While the ram's horns were blowing, the armed men went in front of them, and the rear guard went behind the ark of the Lord.

—Joshua 6:12-13

COMING FULL CIRCLE

God moves in a mysterious way,
His wonders to perform.

—WILLIAM COWPER

What's keeping you awake at night? Hindering your success? Blocking your way at work or home? That's your Jericho.

I remember the first time I visited Jericho, the City of Palms. We crested a mountain, and there it was, spread out like a putting green in the middle of a giant sand trap. Jericho is the world's lowest city in elevation (nearly a thousand feet below sea level), surrounded by the bleak Judean Desert with arid mountains to the east and the Dead Sea to the south.

The secret of its survival is a marvelous aquifer that produces a thousand gallons of water a minute, allowing favorable conditions for irrigation and the growing of wheat, barley, and fruits. Other nearby springs serve as supplements.

That's why Jericho is the oldest continuously-inhabited city on Earth. Today, it's a sprawling Palestinian town on the West Bank, famous for citrus products and Dead Sea cosmetics. Along its modern edges, huge barren mounds of archaeological ruins rise like camels' humps, representing twenty successive settlements going back eleven thousand years.

On the other side of the city, the road to Jerusalem ascends at a sharp rate, twisting through desolate mountains, and the perpendicular sides of the eastern ridges form a natural barrier protecting the Judean highlands. This road represented the best—virtually the only—route into the interior of the land. This was the famous Jericho Road, and its deep ravines inspired David's imagery of the valley of the shadow of death.

The walled city of Jericho stood between Joshua and the route into the interior of the Promised Land—and Jericho wasn't going anywhere. Archaeological evidence suggests it had a double wall on a terraced incline, making it impregnable. But God can pierce the impregnable. He's full of strange techniques. The Lord does things His way, and He delights in devising curious methods to accomplish His work.

The problems in our lives—the intractable ones defying solutions—are areas God has given us as special arenas for His strange grace and mysterious mercy. Victory isn't found in pushing through our own schemes but in cooperating with what He intends to accomplish in His own way and time.

How do we cooperate?

Joy Ridderhof was the founder of Gospel Recordings, a missions organization that now provides language and evangelism tools in thousands of languages. The early days of Gospel Recordings were tough; and as a single career woman, Joy faced loneliness, sickness, dangerous travels, foreign intrigue, and financial crises at every step. One year, Gospel Recordings badly needed to expand its Los Angeles base. Joy and her staff prayed about it for months, and suddenly a site became available. It seemed ideal, and the board authorized a $6,000 deposit. The property cost ten times that much, but Joy, according to her convictions, refused to publicly appeal for funds.

She was in Wheaton, Illinois, as the deadline approached. If $60,000 didn't materialize within a week, the property would be lost along with the $6,000 deposit. Only half the amount was on hand, and Joy's staff called her in crisis. Her laconic instructions were to claim Joshua 3:5 and "follow the Jericho pattern for these remaining seven days and cable the Branch offices to join us."

No other explanation was given, but none was needed. The staff understood. Cables flew around the world: "BUILDING DEADLINE OCTOBER NINTH FOLLOW JERICHO PATTERN NEXT SEVEN DAYS JOSHUA 3:5."

Joy and her staff encircled their Jericho in earnest prayer for seven days. Within the week in an overseas call from London, a British staffer announced an unexpected legacy had just arrived for the ministry, and it was exactly enough to complete the building's purchase. The home staff burst into the Doxology, and Joy Ridderhof continued her speaking tour through Illinois with a new story of God's faithfulness.[28]

Whatever your challenge, claim Joshua 3:5 and follow the Jericho pattern.

SHOFAR, SO GOOD

By faith the walls of Jericho fell down after being marched around by the Israelites for seven days.

—HEBREWS 11:30

According to Joshua's instructions, a contingency of priests and warriors mustered in parade formation—a large military vanguard, followed by seven priests blowing shofars (ram's horns), followed by other priests carrying the ark of the covenant, followed by the rearguard of armed soldiers.

The battalion circled the city every day for six days, marching in total silence except for the mournful, haunting reverberations of the shofars. On the seventh day, they marched around the city seven times.

Early on the seventh day, they started at dawn and marched around the city seven times in the same way. That was the only day they marched around the city seven times. After the seventh time, the priests blew the

ram's horns, and Joshua said to the troops, "Shout! For the Lord has given you the city…."
So the troops shouted, and the ram's horns sounded. When they heard the blast of the ram's horn, the troops gave a great shout, and the wall collapsed. The troops advanced into the city, each man straight ahead, and they captured the city. (Joshua 6:15-20)

Perhaps there are times we can literally march around our Jerichos. Recently, I heard of a godly woman in an overseas location whose ministry center was unfinished. Every night she climbed to the roof and walked around the ramparts, pleading with God for the needed funds and volunteers. Today, the work produced by that center is remarkable.

Our obstacles are God's opportunities, and they must be encircled His way—not necessarily physically but spiritually. Not with platitudes, pessimism, or pop guns but with biblical weapons intended for the pulling down of strongholds (2 Corinthians 10:4).

First, encircle your obstacle with power, power found only in the presence of Him who died and rose again for us. He is as surely in our midst as the ark of the covenant was in the middle of the daily cavalcade around the city.

Second, encircle your obstacle with prayer. Why did the Lord tell them to march in silence, except for the blowing of the shofar? Perhaps it was because He wanted them to pray. The warriors needed to fix their thoughts on the Commander, keeping their hearts tuned to His frequency. Sometimes, the only way to secure the victory is by encircling the problem with prayer. Prayer wings its way from our lips and hearts through the heavens to the very Throne Room of God Himself. Prayer is a commanded activity. God tells us to pray, and He promises to answer.

Third, encircle your obstacle with promises. Pastor Dudley Rutherford wrote, "I believe this notable city met its ultimate demise because a group of faithful men and women placed their focus and trust on the greatness of their God rather than the size of their problem."[29]

The Israelites took the Commander of the Lord's hosts at His word, and, while they didn't know exactly what was going to happen, they knew *He* did. A British preacher named Henry Melvill wrote, "Let us remember that then only can there be hope of success in our endeavors, when we advance, like the Israelites, in a believing temper, using in faith the weapons which God has revealed, and pleading in faith the promises which God has delivered."[30]

Fourth, encircle your obstacle with perseverance. Archaeological ruins suggest the ancient city of Jericho covered about ten acres. A ten-acre square has four sides of about 660 feet. Let's say if the Israelites stayed a few yards outside the walls, then they perhaps covered 700 feet per side, or 2,800 feet. That's just more than a half-mile, so this journey wasn't a very long one. It didn't call for massive strength or a fatiguing struggle. Just consistency. Perseverance.

Fifth, encircle your obstacle with praise. The shofar and the shout of victory permeated the entire operation with praise. Psalm 47:5 says, "God ascends among shouts of joy, the Lord, with the sound of a ram's horn."

When you combine God's powerful presence with prayer, promises, perseverance, and praise, you create a vibration of victory that rattles walls and, with the help of angelic hosts, dislodges stones and demolishes strongholds.

When I was ten or eleven, I went with my mother to her childhood church in the mountains. As I recall, we sat near the front, and as the preacher huffed and puffed, I leaned against the end of the pew and felt drowsy. Suddenly the woman behind me leaped into the air with a blood-curdling shriek. I nearly leaped from my pew too! The woman stepped into the aisle and started dancing and shouting, and a few others whooped and shouted too. I still suffer a bit of post-traumatic stress from the shock of the moment.

But, in retrospect, I haven't personally shouted enough. I'm an introvert, and I don't even shout at ballgames. But one morning, recently, when I got out of bed, having studied Joshua 6, I said aloud at mid-volume, "Praise the Lord!"

The morning after, I walked into the chilly backyard and quoted aloud Psalm 150 in a slightly elevated tone. I'm working on it.

The book of Psalms frequently tells us to try shouting a bit.

- *Let us shout for joy at your victory.* —Psalm 20:5

- *Play skillfully on the strings, with a joyful shout.* —Psalm 33:3

- *Let the whole earth shout joyfully to God!* —Psalm 66:1

- *Happy are the people who know the joyful shout.* —Psalm 89:15

The Palm Sunday crowds shouted, "Hosanna to the Son of David! Blessed is he who comes in the name of the Lord!" (Matthew 21:9).

God Himself shouts. Isaiah 42:13 says, "The Lord advances like a warrior; he stirs up his zeal like a soldier. He shouts, he roars aloud, he prevails over his enemies."

In John 11:43, Jesus shouted with a loud voice, "Lazarus, come out!" And soon He's going to shout again, for 1 Thessalonians 4:16 says, "For the Lord himself will descend from heaven with a shout."

When was the last time you shouted?

Shout to the Lord when you emerge from the wilderness. Shout when the Jordan River parts. Shout when you cross to another stage. Shout when the obstacles block your path. "Let's enter his presence with thanksgiving; let's shout triumphantly to him in song" (Psalm 95:2).

Try it now. It doesn't even have to be very loud, not at first. You can be alone. You don't have to give someone nearby a heart attack.

But it wouldn't hurt to startle the devil, would it?

So let's sing the wondrous love of Jesus, sing His mercy and His grace. Let's encircle our obstacles with biblical faith, shout the victory, and go forward in Jesus' name to possess by faith the promised land God has assigned us for His glory.

For individual and group study materials, including videos and study guides, and for discounts on bulk purchases, visit jordanriverrules.com

EPILOGUE

The funniest thing happened before writing this. After breakfast, I decided to read Joshua 1 through 6 and review this manuscript a final time. I chose a large-print Bible from the bookshelf, sat at my desk, and opened it. But I couldn't find the chapters. They were missing! The Bible went from Deuteronomy 33 to Joshua 7, and I vaguely remembered the person who gave it to me explaining that it was a "second." He bought several copies at a reduced price because of omissions in the printing process.

Check your own copy of the Bible and make sure Joshua 1 through 6 are there—and then put them into practice.

It's been well over a year since Katrina moved out of our Tennessee home and took up residence in the Celestial City. This book has been therapy for me, and I hope it'll be therapeutic for you as well. The other day I stood on the patio and looked into the sky. I thought of my wife, my parents, my miscarried older sibling of whom I know little, and all my friends and family who have already arrived in New Jerusalem.

I didn't shout, but I did exclaim aloud: "I've got people up there!"

You do too. Our days on earth are fleeting, but the Lord knows each of them. Realize He means for you to go forward. Say no to discouragement and yes to strength. Step up to the moment, and find someone to help along the way. Expect God to guide you where you've never been before. Prepare today for tomorrow's wonders, and trust God to turn problems into pathways. Build some monuments. You're not in charge, but remember who is. Encircle obstacles with biblical faith, claim the land—and don't forget to shout the victory.

P.S.

In a 1990 article in *The New York Times* entitled "Believers Score in Battle Over the Battle of Jericho," John Noble Wilford, a Pulitzer Prize-winning science journalist for the newspaper, wrote, "After years of doubt among archaeologists, a new analysis of excavations has yielded a wide range of evidence supporting the biblical account about the fall of Jericho. It may well be true that, in the words of the old spiritual, 'Joshua fit the battle of Jericho, and the walls come tumbling down.'"

Wilford described ceramic remnants, royal scarabs, carbon-14 dating techniques, seismic activity, and archaeological remains, all pointing toward the accuracy of the biblical account. And he quoted Canadian archaeologist Dr. Bryant G. Wood, who concluded, "When we compare the archeological evidence at Jericho with the biblical narrative describing the Israelite destruction of Jericho, we find a quite remarkable agreement."[31]

You're not surprised, are you?

NOTES

1. The bold emphasis in these verses is mine.

2. https://www.brainyquote.com/quotes/lauren_bacall_104647

3. https://www.beulah.edu/alumnispotlight (This link doesn't currently work)

4. William C. Martin, "My Heavenly Father Watches Over Me," 1910. Common domain.

5. Gregory A. Boyd, Present Perfect (Grand Rapids: Zondervan, 2010), 15.

6. Martha Saxton, The Widow Washington (New York: Farrar, Straus and Giroux, 2019), 55.

7. The bold emphasis in these verses is mine.

8. Melvin E. Dieter et al., Five Views on Sanctification (Grand Rapids: Zondervan, 1987), 183.

9. Hudson Taylor's Choice Sayings: A Compilation from His Writings and Addresses (London: China Inland Mission, n.d), 52.

10. I don't recall the professor, but I do seem to recall he was quoting or paraphrasing Major Ian Thomas.

11. Martin Dugard, The Explorers: A Story of Fearless Outcasts, Blundering Geniuses, and Impossible Success (New York: Simon & Schuster, 2014), 12.

12. Martin Dugard, The Explorers: A Story of Fearless Outcasts, Blundering Geniuses, and Impossible Success (New York: Simon & Schuster, 2014), 15-16.

13. David M. Howard, Jr., The New American Commentary: Joshua (Broadman & Holman, 1998), vol. 5, p. 122.

14. John Bunyan, The Pilgrim's Progress (Abbotsford, WI: Aneko Press, 2014), 51-52.

15. https://www.bibleplaces.com/blog/2013/02/picture-of-week-jordan-river-flooding/

16. Journal of a Deputation Sent to the East by the Committee of the Malta Protestant College, in 1849 (London: James Nisbet and Co., 1854), 374.

17. Berton Braley, "At Your Service: The Panama Gang," published in 1912.

18. Oscar C. Eliason, "Got Any Rivers," also known as "God Satisfies," published in 1931.

19. Quoted by L. B. Cowman in Streams in the Desert, in the devotion for February 6, slightly condensed and adapted.

20. Bill March, "How to Cross a River," Backpacker, April-May 1979, 72-73.

21. Theresa Woodson, "Voices of Hope: Breast Cancer Patients Celebrate Their Struggles, Successes, Survival," TCPalm, October 8, 2019,https://www.tcpalm.com/story/specialty-publications/luminaries/2019/10/08/voices-hope-breast-cancer-survivors-share-how-they-dealt-diagnosis-treatment-recovery-and-enjoying-l/3905105002/.

22. Jordan Privett, "Meshell: 'Impossible Is Just I Am Possible,'" Cassville Democrat, December 31, 2019, https://www.cassville-democrat.com/story/2658677.html.

23. Charles Towne, "Life Is Like a River," The Apopka Voice, February 4, 2018, https://theapopkavoice.com/life-like-river/.

24. Richard McLellan, Warriors of Ethiopia (published by Richard J. McLellan, 2006), adapted from chapter 6.

25. Dr. Kevin Moore from his unpublished manuscript, Ink: Your Story and the Power of Pen.

26. In a personal conversation with Larry Bollback and also from "Campfire Stories" by Jodie Sewall in The Experience: Word of Life, Summer 2017, p. 5.

27. D. Steele in Commentary on the Old Testament, Vol. III.-Joshua to II. Samuel. (New York: Nelson & Phillips, 1875), 42.

28. Portions of the story found at https://globalrecordings.net/nl/657.

29. Dudley Rutherford, Walls Fall Down (Nashville: Nelson Books, 2014), 10.

30. Henry Melvill, The Fall of Jericho (London: Francis & John Rivington, 1848), 25.

31. John Noble Wilford, "Believers Score in Battle Over the Battle of Jericho," The New York Times, February 22, 1990, https://www.nytimes.com/1990/02/22/world/believers-score-in-battle-over-the-battle-of-jericho.html.